The Return To G-d Soul Kit

Rae Shagalov

Holy Sparks

Copyright 1999-2015 Rae Shagalov
All Rights Reserved

TERMS OF USE:
Please read carefully.
Thank you for respecting the livelihood of the artist.

Personal and Gift Giving License
All Holy Sparks Art Downloads and Coloring Pages are for personal use only of the buyer of the book. Print out as many as you like for your personal use only, including family members living with you. You may also give printed versions as gifts after you have colored them in or added your own created touches, provided that the credit line on the pages remains intact.

Please do not share these files, post for resale or redistribute via other channels, or copy any part of this book for others or for any other reason without the permission of the author. Contact us at info@holysparks.com for group discounts.

Professional & Extended Use License
Contact us at info@holysparks.com for inquiries for proposed use beyond the Personal License. Discount rates are available for groups, and an Extended License is available for group or professional use. You can order additional copies at: **www.holysparks.com/products/elul-return**

"What's a Soul Like You Doing in a World Like This?"

Some of the Soul Adventures from this "Return to G-d" Soul Kit are an excerpt from Rae Shagalov's full six week program, ***"What's a Soul Like You Doing in a World Like This?"*** This program will guide you step-by-step to create a Personal Development Plan, and help you get *really* clear about who you are and what you're here to do. **If you would like access to the full self-study program,** go to: http://bit.ly/Soul-Plan

---

✌ In Appreciation ✌

To my dear husband, Rabbi Y.Y. Shagalov
To the teachers in whose classes I took these Artnotes: Rabbi Shimon Raichik, Rabbi Elchonon Tauber, Rabbi Reuven Wolf, Rabbi C.Z. Citron, Rabbi Shlomo Holland, Mrs. Etti Rafi, Mrs. Olivia Schwartz, Mrs. Chana Rachel Schusterman, Mrs. Shira Smiles, and Mrs. Chavi Panet.

What Is a Soul Kit?

This Soul Kit is designed to inspire you with beautiful calligraphy Artnotes, quotes, and guided Soul Adventures to help focus on teshuva for 30 days, little by little, step by step. Sometimes, it's hard to do a sincere soul search searching to discover where we have left the path of G-dliness, and what we need to do to return. It is my deep hope that, with G-d's help, *The Return to G-d Soul Kit*, will help you shine a light on your path. For best results, surround yourself with these beautiful Holy Sparks Artnotes as reminders on your walls, in your car, on your fridge – wherever you need an extra boost of light to help you remember that G-d loves you and is waiting for you to return. Make yourself a nice cup of tea, and give yourself a quiet space and time each day to focus on your holy work of refining your soul and reconnecting to G-d through prayer, meditation, and these Soul Adventures.

What is a Soul Adventure?

A Soul Adventure is a creative journey above time and space to explore the vast, fascinating chambers of your own soul and the G-dly hints, echoes, whispers, and holy sparks that are hidden in your innermost self. The prompts and meditations in these Soul Adventures are designed to help you identify and elevate the Holy Sparks in your life, and create a closer relationship with the Master of the Universe. May you be blessed with success and only good things!

Let's Connect!
Facebook.com/soultips
Pinterest.com/holysparks
Twitter.com/holysparks
Youtube.com/holysparksbooks
Instagram.com/holysparks

ೞ How to Use This Soul Kit ೞ

You Know You Should Be Starting the Deep, Inner Work to Prepare for Rosh Hoshanah, But How Should You Begin? What Should You Do? And Who Has Time, Anyway?!!!

Elul is the time to think about what you want to accomplish on Rosh Hoshanah and for the whole year. But, how do you do Teshuvah? And isn't it kind of hard? Now, there's a new, creative way to get into the deep introspective Soul Work! The Return to G-d Soul Kit will help you think outside the box about teshuva.

Download and print for the whole family:
- Interesting Conversation Starters for Your Children
- Creative Ways to Get Deeper into Your Soul Work
- Meditative Coloring Pages
- Art to Put Up All Around Your House to Set the Tone for Elul and Rosh Hoshanah, Yom Kippur and the 10 Days of Awe

This Digital Soul Kit includes:
- 28 beautiful Artnotes to surround yourself with inspiration
- 21 Soul Adventures - a fun, creative way to do introspection!
- 12 Coloring Pages for the whole family to discuss how to make good life changes

For best results, print this whole document from your color printer. You can do the Soul Adventures in order, out of order, more than once – however it works best for you to help you explore your inner world, do an accounting of your soul, and connect to G-d.

Coloring is a very relaxing, peaceful, meditative activity. As you color in the pages, contemplate the Artnotes thoughts on them and try to internalize them. If you're doing this as a family activity, discuss the ideas while you color them in together. Afterwards, hang up these beautiful family treasures around your home to set a wonderful holy mood for Rosh Hashannah, Yom Kippur, and the 10 Days of Awe.

Feel free to draw outside the lines, doodle, or crumple it up and print out a new one. Sometimes teshuva (and life!) is like that. Enjoy!

THE RETURN TO G-D SOUL KIT
HOW TO DO THE SPIRITUAL WORK OF ELUL

INTRODUCTION

The Hebrew month of Elul, which precedes Rosh Hashanah, the Jewish New Year, is the last month of the Jewish year. It has a very special spiritual energy for fixing past mistakes, clearing out the dust and stains of actions and behaviors that don't reflect who we really want to be, and creating a new closeness with G-d.

> "The winds of Elul are blowing." The very air is charged with holiness."

The month of Elul, says Rabbi Schneur Zalman of Liadi, is when the King is in the field. The King's usual place is in the capital city, in the royal palace. Only a few very special people are allowed into the King's throne room. Anyone wishing to approach the King must first dress up, pass through many gates and halls, and get permission from all of the ministers and guards in the palace, and even then, the King is often stern.

For the month of Elul, G-d becomes like a King who is passing through the fields of His kingdom as He travels back to the palace. At such times, anyone can approach Him; the King receives them all with a smiling face. The farmer in his dusty clothes has even more access to the King than the ministers of the royal court when the King is in the palace.

When the farmer sees the King in his field, does he keep on plowing? Does he behave as if this were just another ordinary workday in the fields? No, he stops what he's doing, brushes himself off, and goes to speak to the King. When the King is in the field, He is easier to approach and receives everyone with a smile. You come as you are. You don't experience the glory of the palace. You don't receive an invitation. You make the effort to go see Him on your own, and a good and sweet year results.

In Elul, G-d lowers Himself to our level. We come close to Him in the field as one greets a Beloved Friend.

Elul is not a month of ordinary days; it is a time of great adventure for the soul.

It is a time to pause, brush off our dusty souls, and take time to greet and speak to the king.

Elul is a time to increase our daily introspection, prayers, Torah study, and generosity.

"The winds of Elul are blowing." The very air is charged with holiness. We might still be in the field of our everyday lives, but the field has become a holier place.

TESHUVA
RETURNING TO G-D

The Four "R's" of Teshuva

1. **Recognize that what you did was wrong.**
2. **Regret what you did wholeheartedly.**
3. **Resolve not to do it again.**
4. **Refrain from making the same mistake when faced with the same situation.**

"Teshuva" means "Return" – returning to the path of G-dliness. Our Sages teach us that when we do Teshuva, we rectify our mistakes. We actually fix and uplift all previous mistakes of the same nature and restore the holiness of our being. In this way, bit by bit, we restore the entire world to holiness.

Every person has the strength to change. Choose something small--one thing you would like to change in yourself. Work on it every day for a whole year. Pray and meditate every day and ask G-d to help you change this one thing. If you wronged another person, take courage and ask the person you have hurt to forgive you. If that's not possible ask G-d to forgive you with your whole heart.

Don't become discouraged. The Harsh Inner Critic sometimes says, "Who are you fooling? You'll never change! Don't even bother to try – you've failed a million times before!" Tell your Inner Voice: "Thank you for your opinion, but I can change, and with G-d's help, I will change." Every single little bit of Teshuva counts. Never underestimate what you can accomplish with your effort!

Teshuva can be done at any time of the year, in any moment – even in one's last moments. It's easiest to do teshuva a little bit at a time, at bedtime each night, weekly before the Sabbath, or before each new month begins. It's easier to keep your house in good repair by fixing things as they break, instead of waiting till the house falls down in disrepair, and so it is with the care and maintenance of your soul.

ב"ה

Teshuva

The 4 Steps of Teshuva

- **Recognize** that what you did was wrong.
- **Regret** what you did wholeheartedly.
- **Resolve** not to do it ever again.
- **Refrain** from doing that thing the next time you are faced with the same situation!

THE LONGER YOU REFRAIN, THE LESS THAT TEMPTATION WILL BOTHER YOU, UNTIL EVENTUALLY IT CEASES TO BE A DIFFICULT ISSUE.

Holy Sparks
© 2010 Rae Shagalov
WWW.HOLYSPARKS.ORG

SOUL ADVENTURE #1

Take 5 minutes today just to enjoy the inner journey. Contemplate your relationship with G-d and the pleasure both you and G-d feel from your effort to come closer through your teshuva.

SOUL ADVENTURE #2
WAKE UP FROM THE DREAM

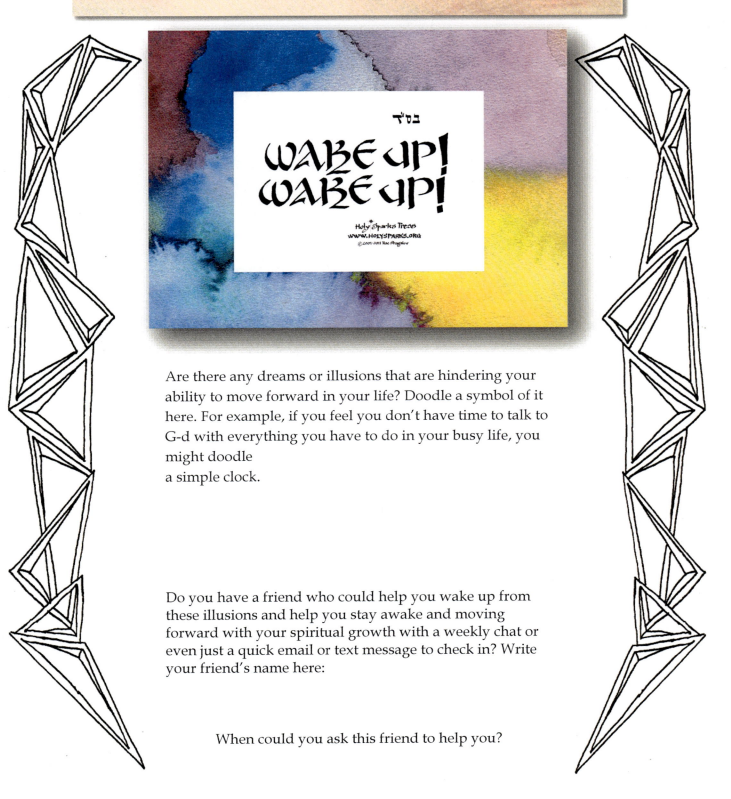

Are there any dreams or illusions that are hindering your ability to move forward in your life? Doodle a symbol of it here. For example, if you feel you don't have time to talk to G-d with everything you have to do in your busy life, you might doodle
a simple clock.

Do you have a friend who could help you wake up from these illusions and help you stay awake and moving forward with your spiritual growth with a weekly chat or even just a quick email or text message to check in? Write your friend's name here:

When could you ask this friend to help you?

בס"ד

We all want to be good, but we must wake up!

TESHUVA
The Facing Days of Din

JUST OPEN ONE LITTLE OPENING, THIS BIG, THE SIZE OF A NEEDLE, AND I WILL OPEN FOR YOU A GREAT OPENING.

I am a friend to my friend and my friend gives my friendship back to me.

WAKE UP! WAKE UP!

Wake up from the beautiful dream of the whole year! IF YOU RECEIVED A COURT SUMMONS IN THE MAIL, YOU WOULD FEEL A SHOCK OF FEAR. YOU WOULD CALL THE BEST LAWYERS. YOU WOULD CALL ALL YOUR FRIENDS AND ASK FOR THEIR ADVICE. YOU WOULD CAREFULLY GO THROUGH ALL OF YOUR ACCOUNTS TO DETERMINE THE TRUTH OF YOUR SITUATION.

IT'S ELUL!

YOUR SUMMONS HAS COME IN THE MAIL! FEEL THE SHOCK! CALL YOUR LAWYERS! CALL YOUR FRIENDS! GO THROUGH YOUR ACCOUNTS TODAY! DETERMINE THE TRUTH OF YOUR SITUATION! WHO ARE YOUR LAWYERS? **Your mitzvahs** WHO ARE YOUR FRIENDS? **Your good actions!**

Sometimes, a person refuses to wake up. What happens? His friend shakes him awake so he won't be late for an important engagement. WE HAVE A CHOICE. WE CAN WAKE UP ON OUR OWN, EARLY, AND PREPARE OURSELVES CAREFULLY; OR WE CAN PULL THE BLANKET OVER OUR HEADS, REFUSE TO WAKE UP, AND BE SHAKEN AWAKE BY OUR GREATEST FRIEND IN THE WORLD...

More than we keep Shabbos, Shabbos keeps us. WE HAVE TO KEEP SHABBOS 100% - NOT 95%, NOT 99% - **100%**
Rebbitzen Chavi Panet 5758
Rosh Chodesh Elul
TORAH OHR ✦✦ LOS ANGELES

When a woman lights Shabbos lights and davens for those she loves with tears, AN ANGEL COLLECTS HER PRECIOUS TEARS AND BRINGS THEM TO THE THRONE OF GLORY AND SAYS TO HAKADOSH BARUCH HU, "LOOK AT THE PRECIOUS JEWELS I HAVE BROUGHT TO YOU, THE TEARS OF A YIDDISCHE MOTHER." T.69

Holy Sparks Press
www.holysparks.org
© 2001-2011 Rae Shagalov

SOUL ADVENTURE #3
TAKE 5 MINUTES OUT OF YOUR BUSY LIFE TODAY AND ASK YOURSELF…

ב"ה

At Rosh Hoshana the pain will come shooting out of our hearts. **But thankfulness should also come screaming out of our hearts.**

If you have been hurt, forgive and go on.

Take courage and ask the people you have hurt to forgive you.

TAKE COURAGE AND LIVE!

Don't be afraid to do teshuva. Don't be afraid to change. Don't be afraid to take the next step.

Tomorrow is going to be a tomorrow whether you show up or not, so why not jump into tomorrow with your whole heart?

Every person has the strength to change. When the neshama does a sin and doesn't do teshuva, the soul feels like it doesn't belong; like a person who goes to a wedding, even though he wasn't invited. But when you do teshuva, all of G-d's love pours down on you and you feel like an honored guest. You feel like you belong.

May our prayers give us Life.

NEVER GIVE UP!

Do a little bit of teshuva every day.

Selichos 5758 25 Elul 26

How many days of this year can you say you really lived? How many days did you smile?

How did you live this year?

It takes courage to make Teshuva. Every one of us is a leader. Every one of us is the leader of our own lives. This is YOUR Rosh Hoshana! Take charge of your teshuva. **A little bit is also good.** Change one small thing before the end of this year. The yetzer hara is so smart. The evil urge tells you, if it isn't a big thing, don't bother. Tell the yetzer hara, "I will change this small thing first. Later I will change that big thing for extra credit."

Forgive everyone!

Rabbi Tauber

Nine days to Rosh Hoshana: Take charge!

Holy Sparks Press
www.holysparks.org
© 2001-2011 Rae Shagalov

SOUL ADVENTURE #4
ASK G-D TO FORGIVE YOU FOR THE THINGS YOU'VE DONE WRONG.

On index cards, or small slips of paper, write or draw a symbol of the things for which you want to ask G-d's forgiveness. Put the little notes in a bowl, box or bag. Draw them out one at a time, and ask G-d to forgive you for each one. Decorate the container to look festive like a present, because by doing this inner work, you are giving a gift to G-d.

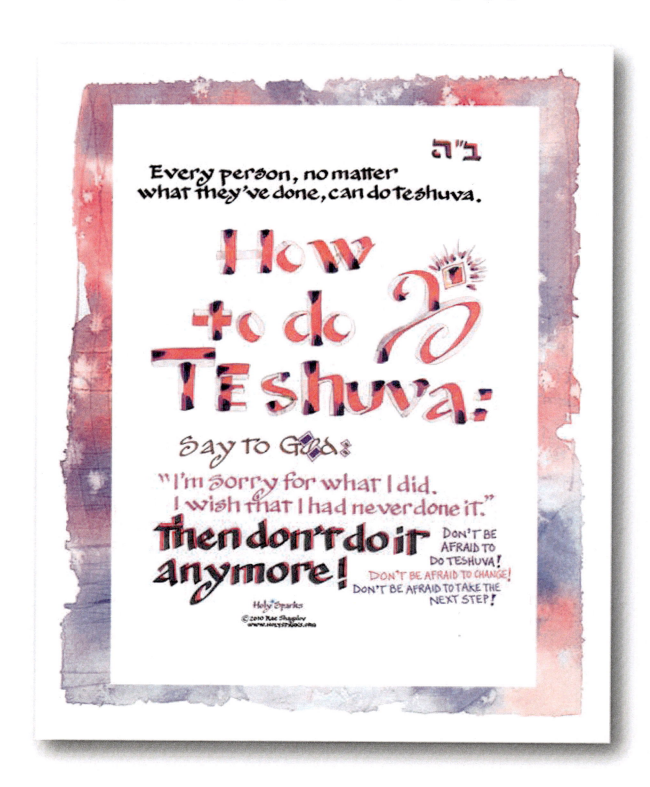

SOUL ADVENTURE #5
ASK THE PEOPLE IN YOUR LIFE, WHOM YOU MIGHT HAVE HURT, TO FORGIVE YOU. JUST SAY…

Color this page, cut it out, and write a personal message on the back to someone you would like to forgive you. Then, give or mail it to the person.

SOUL ADVENTURE #6
TAKE CHARGE OF YOUR TRIGGERS

1. What is something that often triggers a difficult-to-control, negative reaction from you? Write or doodle it below.

2. What is one small thing you could do to begin to become proactive and take conscious charge of your reaction to that situation?

3. What is a new positive trigger you could create to replace the old negative one? This might be a word, a song, a tap, or some other physical or verbal reminder.

SOUL ADVENTURE #7
CHANGE ONE SMALL THING

1. Choose one thing you would like to change in yourself this year.
2. Write it in the frame below.
3. Post it where you will see it every day to remind you. At the beginning of each month, take it down and decorate it to revive your attention to it.

ב"ה

Teshuva: The Challenge of SELF RECREATION

The truest reality is in the thoughts of the heart of G☼d

In Tishrei the world was conceived; in Nissan the world was actualized.

Where does Teshuva take place? In the heart and will of man.

Things are alive because they exist in the heart and will of Hashem.

If for one second G☼d were to cease thinking of us in his heart, in that moment we would cease to exist.

My heart is in the heart of G☼d. My will is in the will of G☼d. When I do a sin, I take my heart out of the heart of G☼d. I take myself away from the will of G☼d. I put my life in danger. Every sin cuts a nick in the cord that binds me to the womb of the will of Hashem. Every sin takes away a little bit of life.

I am my choices

The self is the culmination of the choices one makes with one's free will. If one can choose to take oneself away from the will of G☼d, one can also choose to come close again to G☼d. **This is Teshuva.** Teshuva is not eliminating desire. Teshuva is facing the desire with a new heart, with a strong heart to resist the desire.

On Yom Kippur we are given a great pool of Rachamim. We need only immerse ourselves in this mikveh of mercy with a new heart.

If you don't rebirth yourself in your heart, you cannot rebirth yourself in your actions. If you are sorry but nothing changes, there is no teshuva. You must make a new heart. But it must really be a new heart. How do we make a new heart? Through vidoy, confession. Vidoy is understanding the cause, the root, the motivation for being tempted to move out of the heart of G☼d. The tears, the words, the beating of the chest are not enough. You must understand with your heart.

From my heart to the heart of G☼d

My heart is bigger than any temptation

Rabbi Holland   Anshe Emes

Holy Sparks
www.holysparks.org
©2001-2012 Rae Shagalov

7 Tishrei 5758

Be like a baby...
A baby does three things: he laughs. He cries. He is always moving. Be joyful; cry and nag Hashem until you get what you want, to be close to Hashem. And always keep moving spiritually, higher and and higher.

I don't want your olam haba. I don't want your gan eden. I just want you.

A woman had an account in a store. Every month she came into the store to pay off her bill. One month, the time came to pay the bill but the woman had no money. She went to the store and told the man when more money came, she would pay the bill. Since she came every month he trusted her and gave her more from his store. Every day we buy things from G‑d's store. We buy breath, we buy legs for walking, we buy good health and livelihood. On Rosh Hashana the bill comes. We are given the month of Elul to make the Cheshbon Hanefesh, an accounting of the soul. What is the money we use to pay the bill? Torah and mitzvahs. Isn't it better to pay cash?

Chai Elul 5759 The birthday of the Baal Shem Tov and the Alte Rebbe.
Mrs. Etti Rafi

10.3

בס״ד

What do you do when a well goes dry? Dig a little deeper.

When your life force dries out, you have to dig deeper in your soul to draw forth a flow of living waters, to draw forth Divine energy into your soul and into creation.

The sun is always shining, but when a cloud covers it, we cannot see its rays. Our sins create a cloud of unholiness. When we do Teshuvah, the wind blows the cloud away from the Divine light.

Reach the place in your soul that is beyond the damage, and draw the waters from there to repair the damage.

How do you reach beyond the damage to the part of your soul that is pure? Meditate: Have compassion on your soul! This will help you

Return to The Innocence of the Soul

This is the level of Faith. Your soul cries out from the center of its being!

Reach to your inner, inner self.

Are you giving life to Klippah?

When we sin, we pierce the Shechina and allow the Klippa to nurse from it and draw from its holy energy. Klippa is the force of evil.

When we sin, we allow unholiness to wrap itself around our soul. How do we remove the unholiness?

First, patch up the holes, then return the Shechina to her rightful place.

www.holysparks.org
© 2001-2013 Rae Shagalov

Rabbi Reuven Wolf Tanya Iggres Hateshuva

16.88

SOUL ADVENTURE #8
TODAY, DIG A LITTLE DEEPER IN YOUR TESHUVA.
**In what area could you be a little more responsible?
Write it in the frame below.**

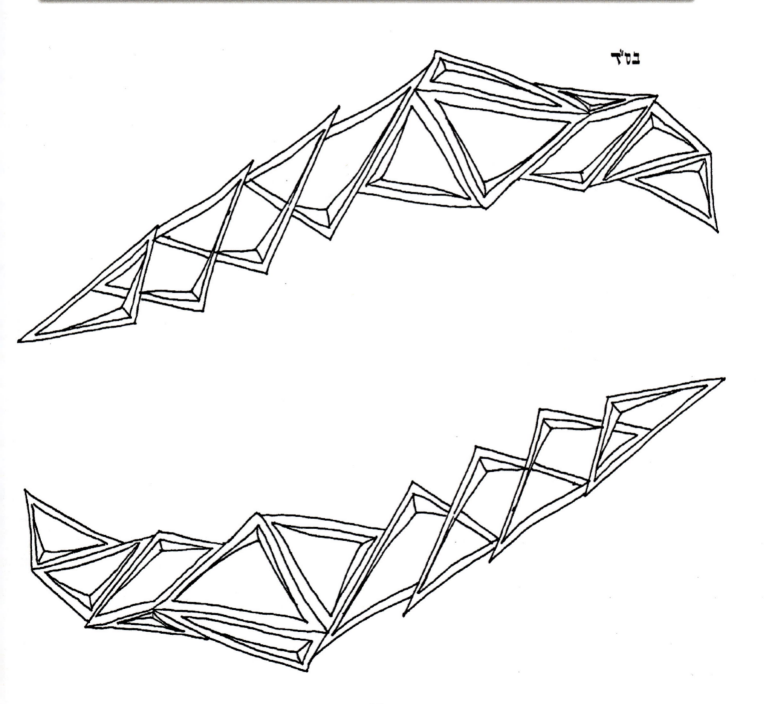

The light of G-d shines on the person who does teshuva. ב"ה

The problem is not the mistake. The problem is not taking responsibility for the mistake

Excuses are the way we avoid making Teshuva.

G-d doesn't expect us to be perfect. G-d just wants us to say, "I'm sorry for what I did."

HOW MANY DAYS WERE YOU LOVING? HOW MANY DAYS WERE YOU KIND? HOW MANY DAYS WERE YOU ANGRY? HOW MANY DAYS DID YOU REALLY ACCOMPLISH ANYTHING?

Instead of wasting time, **Live it!**

"What am I doing wrong that I could change? How could I become a better person?" SIT BY YOURSELF AND ASK HASHEM "HOW DO YOU WANT ME TO CHANGE?"

Let G-d in!

Pray that G-d will help us, especially in Eretz Yisrael!

In difficult times, Hashem is telling us: Talk to me!

This is good. This is not. You choose!

If you want, you'll do.

Kesser, the crown is curiosity. Curiosity brings wisdom.

HOW MANY DAYS OF THIS YEAR CAN YOU SEE YOU REALLY LIVED?

If you don't ask, you won't change. THE QUESTION ITSELF BRINGS ABOUT CHANGE.

Peace takes wisdom. AND WE LACK THAT WISDOM.

Just change one thing this year. Focus on it all year. MANY THINGS WILL CHANGE IN YOUR LIFE AND YOU WILL INFLUENCE OTHERS.

Rabbi Elchonon Tauber

Holy Sparks
www.HOLYSPARKS.ORG
©2001-2012 Rae Shagalov

40 days of Teshuva

16.55

SOUL ADVENTURE #9
CHANGE YOUR CHOICES

Some of the choices we make in life are things we've settled for, or settled into, after we've forgotten or given up on what we really wanted. Some of our choices are the opposite of what we really want or should want for the level of greatness we are striving to achieve. Choose a choice you've made in life that you want to change.

1. What you really want:

2. What you are doing instead of what you really want:

3. The first small step of change:

> EVERY CHANGE WE MAKE,
> NO MATTER HOW GREAT,
> BEGINS WITH A SINGLE SMALL STEP.

SOUL ADVENTURE #10
IF YOU WERE A TINY BIT MORE COURAGEOUS, WHAT COULD BE YOUR NEXT STEP?

ב"ה

THE WORK OF ELUL IS TESHUVA AND ACCOUNTING OF THE SOUL.

THE TIME OF THE 13 ATTRIBUTES OF MERCY.

Holy Sparks
© 2010 Rae Shagalov
www.HOLYSPARKS.ORG

AWAKENING FROM BELOW

THE KING IN THE FIELD — ELUL

AWAKEN AND TURN TO YOUR BELOVED

THE WORK OF TISHREI IS TO ACCEPT HASHEM AS OUR KING.

AWAKENING FROM ABOVE

ROSH HASHANA & YOM KIPPUR TISHREI — THE KING IN THE PALACE.

WHEN THE KING IS IN HIS PALACE, YOU DRESS IN YOUR BEST, YOU MAKE AN APPOINTMENT AND IF YOU ARE LUCKY, YOU ARE ADMITTED TO THE FABULOUS, IMPRESSIVE CHAMBERS OF THE KING WHICH INSPIRE LOVE AND AWE IN YOU.

WHY DO WE BLOW SHOFAR DURING ELUL? IF THE SHOFAR AWAKENS US TO FEAR, WHY DO WE BLOW SHOFAR WHEN THE KING IS SMILING IN THE FIELD?

AHAVA, LOVE IS AN AWAKENING, A REVELATION FROM ABOVE, AN APPRECIATION OF ALL THAT THE ABISHTER GIVES US.

Y'ERA, FEAR IS AN AWAKENING FROM BELOW. WE ACCEPT THE AUTHORITY OF THE KING OVER US AND TREMBLE AT HIS MIGHT. IF WE DID NOT ACCEPT HIS AUTHORITY, WE WOULD NOT FEEL THE FEAR. THIS IS OUR WORK IN TISHREI.

When the king is in the field,

HE IS EASIER TO APPROACH. YOU COME AS YOU ARE. YOU DON'T EXPERIENCE THE GLORY OF THE PALACE. YOU DON'T RECEIVE AN INVITATION. YOU MAKE THE EFFORT TO GO TO SEE HIM ON YOUR OWN. THIS IS AWAKENING FROM BELOW.

We work to Arouse the level of awe in Tishrei, to accept Hashem as our King.

In Elul, the King lowers Himself to our level. We come close to Him in the field as one greets a beloved friend.

The King smiles and encourages us to come closer.

HOW DO WE COME CLOSER? WE SEE WHERE WE HAVE ERRED THROUGH THE YEAR. WE RESOLVE TO CHANGE, BECAUSE WE LOVE THE KING. BUT LOVE IS NOT ENOUGH. WE MUST ALSO FEAR THE MIGHT OF THE KING SO THAT WE WILL BE AFRAID TO REBEL AGAINST HIM. THIS IS **AVODAH SHLEMA, COMPLETE SERVICE.**

※ 4 י'S = 40 DAYS TILL YOM KIPPUR   HASHEM IN EACH WORD.

Heard from: Rabbi Raichik

MA'AMER OF THE REBBE FOR ROSH CHODESH ELUL 5758 7:65

SOUL ADVENTURE #11
HEALING REGRETS

A regret is a hole, a gap in the heart where something important is missing. Just as a hole in a boat will cause the boat to sink, regrets evoke in us a sinking feeling, a feeling of loss. If we don't take action to correct the lack that regret leaves behind, the vessel of holiness we are building with our positive actions, begins to leak. When we use regret to do teshuva, we remove the unholiness that has wrapped itself around the soul, and then we can purify ourselves.

On the left, write or draw a symbol of something you regret. For each regret you feel, write or doodle a symbol of something in the right column (no matter how small) that you can do this week to take positive action to correct the feeling of loss. Then do it! Take a moment to feel the strength that this positive action restores to you. If you feel, for whatever reason, that you can't do anything to repair the regret, write down any positive thing that may have come from it, such as drawing out your inner strength or developing new skills. If you need more room, use another sheet of paper.

If only I had or had not...	Positive Action or Positive Result

ב"ה

The heart gets excited and wants to get close.

It feels the Infinite Light and gets excited.

WHEN WE CONTEMPLATE HOW GREAT G-D IS, AND HOW COMPLETELY UNATTAINABLE AND UNGRASPABLE G-D IS, OUR SOUL GETS EXCITED AND YEARNS FOR ITS CONNECTION TO G-D.

The yearning for G-dliness brings us closer to G-d.

ס EREV ROSH CHODESH 5766 **Rabbi Y.Y. Shagalov** ♡ 20.21

SOUL ADVENTURE #12
CONSISTENCY

In what area of your spiritual life can you be more consistent?

ב"ד

≈ AROUSAL FROM ABOVE ≈

AS WE LIVE IN ELUL
SO WE WILL LIVE THE REST OF THE YEAR.

◆ **CONSISTENCY** ◆
IS ONE OF THE PRIMARY SPIRITUAL SECRETS OF THE UNIVERSE. CHOOSE ONE AREA IN WHICH TO IMPROVE. WORK ON IT CONSISTENTLY AT THE SAME TIME EVERY DAY.

≈ AROUSAL FROM BELOW ≈
OUR YEARNING AND PRAYER AROUSES G*D'S LOVE FOR US.

G*dliness is most accessible to us in the month of Elul.

THROUGH
◆ TORAH STUDY
◆ PRAYER &
◆ DEEDS OF LOVINGKINDNESS
◆ TZEDAKAH
◆ TESHUVAH

THE KING IS IN THE FIELD

≈ CIRCUMCISION OF THE HEART ≈
WE MUST TURN OUR HEARTS OF STONE TO HEARTS OF FLESH.

EVERY JEW HAS THE POWER TO GIVE A BLESSING • MAY YOUR BLESSINGS BE BLESSED!

MAY WE BE BLESSED WITH THE STRENGTH TO DO WHAT OUR SOUL LONGS TO DO.

AND WITH THE STRENGTH TO SAY NO TO THAT WHICH IS NOT OURS TO DO. MAY WE ALL HAVE WHAT WE NEED.

Heard from: Olivia Schwartz
Bel Air Farbrengen 11 Elul 5757

4.72

Holy Sparks Press
www.HOLYSPARKS.ORG
©2001-2011 Rae Shagalov

SOUL ADVENTURE #13
PUT GUILT TO WORK.

Uncomfortable guilty feelings are signals that something is wrong and some action needs to be taken. If we feel guilty and don't act to change what is wrong, the guilt could turn into action-suppressing depression or avoidance.

Is there anything you feel guilty about? For every guilty feeling, write down something you could do tomorrow to correct what you've done wrong. Then do it! Feel the new energy that this positive action restores to you. If you truly feel there is nothing you can do about the situation, then ask G-d to forgive you and guide you in making up for your mistake.

---

1. I feel guilty that:

2. This is what I should have done:

3. This is what I could do tomorrow to correct it:

---

1. I feel guilty that:

2. This is what I should have done:

3. This is what I could do tomorrow to correct it:

SOUL ADVENTURE #14
MAKE THE GOOD EVEN BETTER.
What is one thing you are already doing well?
How could you improve upon it and do it
in an even more special or beautiful way?
Write or doodle it below.

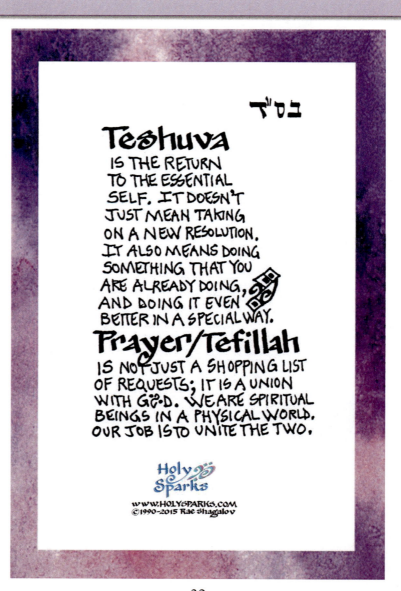

SOUL ADVENTURE #15
Recovering Essence: Refining Your Character Traits
"My G-d, the soul you have placed within me is pure."

We each have a spark of G-dliness in us that is completely pure. No matter what mistakes we have made, this pure place in us, our soul, can never be spoiled. But sometimes it gets covered up by the materialism of this world and needs to be cleaned out. How do we do this? We re-establish our connection to our essence, to the place where we are connected to G-d by shedding the personalities and misdeeds which separate us from G-d. These negative actions and qualities are like rocks and sticks that dam up a stream and prevent the pure water from reaching the fields. G-d's blessings hover above us waiting to pour down on us but first we have to clear out the channel of blessing.

1. What is attached to you that is *not* you? List it below and let it go!

2. Choose one area in which you would like to improve & strengthen your character:

3. List below various ways that you can improve this trait throughout this year:

4. What are other new qualities you would like to integrate into your character?

SOUL ADVENTURE #16
WRITE A LETTER TO G-D

Write a letter to G-d. Include all of your gratitude, doubts, needs, fears, regrets, and all of your struggles and the things you are trying to improve in your life. Talk to G-d whenever you feel discouraged and use your letter to begin your holy conversation.

Did you daven (pray) today? DID YOU TALK TO G-D TODAY? ב"ה

What is G-d asking of you?

ALL YOU NEED IS THE GATE OF TESHUVA TO OPEN. AS SOON AS YOU ENTER THE GATE, YOU ARE BACK.

JUST TO LOVE G-D AND FEAR G-D AND WALK IN G-D'S WAYS! WHAT IS THIS "JUST?" THIS IS NOT EXACTLY A TINY, LITTLE REQUEST. "EVERYTHING IS FROM HEAVEN EXCEPT FEAR OF HEAVEN."

Fear is the gate to G-d.

ALL OF OUR SPIRITUAL QUALITIES ARE A GIFT FROM G-D, EXCEPT THE FEAR OF G-D. THIS WE HAVE TO CHOOSE FOR OURSELVES. THEN THE OTHER GIFTS FLOW.

THE YETZER HARA STUFFS UP OUR HEART. THIS IS WHY WE ARE TOLD TO CIRCUMCISE OUR HEARTS. THE YETZER HARA HAS 100 STOP SIGNS. THE 100 BLESSINGS WE SAY EVERY DAY UNSTOPS THESE STOP SIGNS.

First break your heart, then pray with joy.

HOW DO YOU DO TESHUVA? YOU HAVE TO REACH BEYOND TIME TO A PLACE THAT IS TIMELESS. YOU HAVE TO REACH DEEP TO A PLACE BEYOND YOUR NATURE. YOU HAVE TO GO BACK BEFORE YOU MADE THE SIN AND FIX YOURSELF THERE. TESHUVA WAS MADE BEFORE THE WORLD WAS CREATED. YOU HAVE TO RISE TO THE LEVEL OF WORLD BEFORE CREATION.

What is wholeness?

WHEN YOU FEEL IN YOUR HEART WHAT YOU KNOW IN YOUR HEAD AND YOU KNOW IN YOUR HEAD WHAT YOU FEEL IN YOUR HEART AND YOU DO WHAT YOU KNOW AND FEEL IS RIGHT.

On Shabbos, the whole world is exalted.

Worse than the evil itself, is the joy of evil.

THERE IS A MIDRASH THAT BEFORE MOSES CAME DOWN WITH THE TABLETS THE FIRST TIME, HE HAD A TUG-OF-WAR WITH G-D. HE PULLED THE TABLETS AWAY FROM G-D, THEN CAME DOWN THE MOUNTAIN AND SMASHED THEM. WHY? NOT BECAUSE THE PEOPLE MADE THE GOLDEN CALF, BUT BECAUSE THEY WERE DANCING AROUND IT.

Rabbi Chaim Citron   Parshas Eikev July 29, 5759 9.66

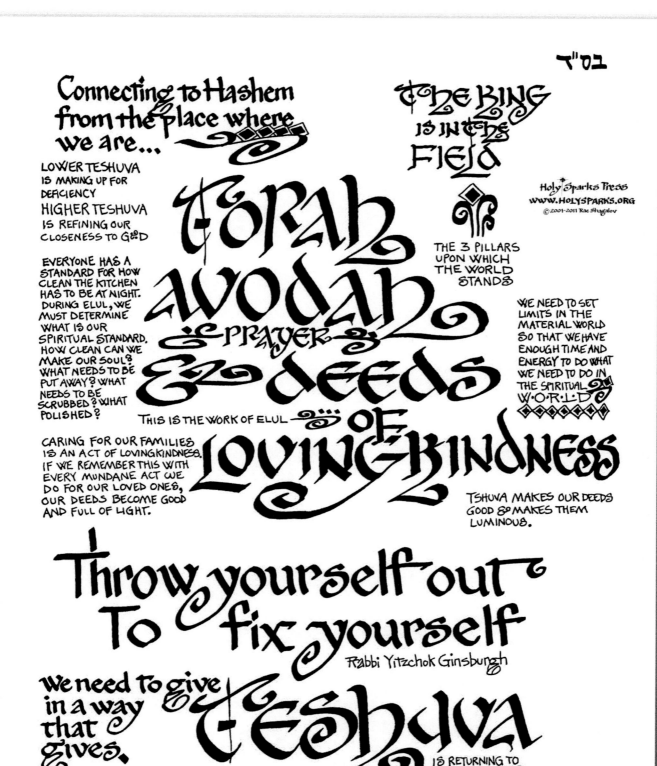

בס"ד

Teshuva

The person who fails to do teshuva feels inadequate & feels like he does not belong in this world.

When a person does teshuva the name of Hashem shines on that person and gives him the strength and courage to face the challenges of life.

Eliyah

We all feel inadequate at times. The more we do teshuva, the more confident we feel. The more we do teshuva, the more we understand ourselves and others. The more we meditate, the closer we come to Hashem and the more intuitive we become.

If you want to be a happy person count your blessings

Just have the courage to say:

When we meditate daily we remember better all of our days. Teshuva becomes much easier because we are fixing as we go along.

Please help me to stop making the same mistake.

I really regret what I did.

OOPS! Master of the Universe I goofed.

Heard from: **Rabbi Tauber**

Sometimes it is so hard to say "I'm sorry" because we don't want to face how wrong we are.

I'm sorry what I did.
Please forgive me
Please help me fix my mistake.

Holy Sparks Press
www.holysparks.org
© 2001-2011 Rae Shagalov

SOUL ADVENTURE #17
SPIRITUAL ACCOUNTING

List your Blessings and Mistakes from this year. Assign an intuitive value to each one. Add the Blessings values and subtract the Mistakes. How did your "balance" come out? How much teshuva do you "owe" to G-d?

Blessings	Mistakes

SOUL ADVENTURE #18
STRETCH YOUR VESSEL

What are some ways that you could create a vessel to receive more of G-d's blessings for you? What good deed or spiritual practice could you commit to for 30 days? Write it in the frame below.

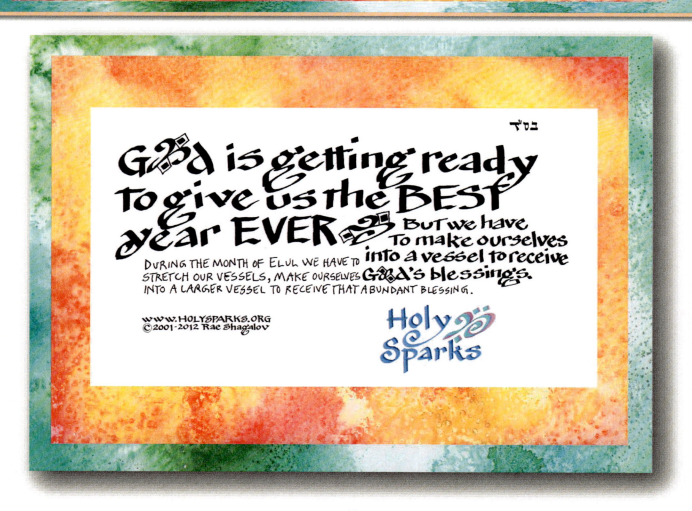

G-d is getting ready to give us the BEST year EVER! But we have to make ourselves into a vessel to receive G-d's blessings. During the month of Elul we have to stretch our vessels, make ourselves into a larger vessel to receive that abundant blessing.

www.holysparks.org
©2001-2012 Rae Shagalov

Holy Sparks

SOUL ADVENTURE #19
YOUR BEST YEAR EVER!

What would your "Best Year Ever" look like? Feel like? Sound like? Describe it in words and pictures below.

SOUL ADVENTURE #20
BREAK THE CHAIN WITH FORGIVENESS!

Is there someone in your life you find it hard to forgive? Forgive and move on! You may feel this person is not worthy of being forgiven, but you are worthy of being a forgiving person. The act of forgiveness will heal your soul and help you move forward into a happier life. The Aramaic word for forgive literally means to "untie." Untie the bindings and loosen yourself from that person's misdeed. Forgiving is freeing yourself from the chain of pain that connects you to that person. The anger you feel toward the person who hurt you harms you, not the other. It takes up valuable space in your emotions that could be used to help and heal.

Take a piece of paper and cut it into strips. You're going to make a paper chain like you did when you were a child. On one strip, write the name of the person who hurt you. On the other strips write what they did and how you felt about it. Glue the ends of each strip together, interlocking them into a chain. When it is complete, tear it apart into little bits and discard the pieces. In your meditation today, ask G-d to help you forgive this person and move onward into more peaceful feelings.

SOUL ADVENTURE #21
Make It a Good and Sweet Year!
What is something you could do to make this a good and sweet year for someone else? Write it in the frame below.

❦ Glossary ❧

Abishter	The One Above
Cheshbon Hanefesh	Accounting of the Soul
Din	Judgment
Gan Eden	Garden of Eden
Ha Kadosh Baruch Hu	The Blessed Holy One
Mitzvahs	Commandments (that connect us to G-d)
Neshama	Soul
Olam Haba	The World to Come
Rosh Chodesh	The new moon of the new month
Rosh Hoshannah	The Jewish New Year
Shabbos	Shabbat or the Sabbath
Shofar	Ram's Horn
Teshuva	Return – returning to the path of G-dliness
Tishrei	The first month in the Hebrew calendar that follows Elul
Tzedakah	Charity
Yiddishe	Jewish

❧ Connect with Rae Shagalov ❧

Sign up to receive free art, coloring pages and Rae's Soul Tips newsletter! Go to: www.holysparks.com

Let's Connect!
Facebook.com/soultips
Pinterest.com/holysparks
Twitter.com/holysparks
Youtube.com/holysparksbooks
Instagram.com/holysparks

❧ About Holy Sparks ❧

Holy Sparks is dedicated to spreading the light of authentic Jewish spirituality and wisdom. Holy Sparks provides and promotes Jewish knowledge, awareness and practice as it applies to people of all faiths and nationalities, regardless of affiliation or background. Holy Sparks helps spiritual seekers, particularly the Jewish people, and others who are looking for inspiration and encouragement, to discover and fulfill their individual talents and potential for service to G-d and mankind, through increasing in acts of goodness, kindness, and holiness.

❧ About Rae Shagalov ❧

Rae Shagalov is a Jewish artist, author, publisher, master calligrapher, and lifelong learner of Torah, currently living in Los Angeles, who has been developing and refining her craft for over 30 years. In her sketchbooks is a rare and extraordinary record of a Jewish artist's spiritual journey through time. Holy sparks is in the process of publishing more than 3,000 pages of Rae's lively and engaging calligraphy Artnotes that contain the most amazing Jewish wisdom from hundreds of Torah, chassidus, and kabbalah classes on every major them in Judaism, from Jewish masters in the United States and Israel. These Artnotes and coloring pages are excerpts from Rae's sketchbook journals.

There's a Holy Spark in each of us that's hidden very well; when it's revealed, we make our world a place where G-d can dwell.

✣ More Books by Rae Shagalov ✤

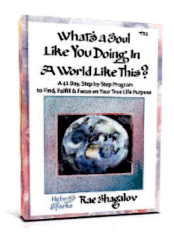

Find and fulfill your purpose in life in just 6 weeks with this art-filled e-book:

What's a Soul Like You Doing in a World Like This?
Find out more about it here: http://bit.ly/Soul-Plan

**Prepare for Passover with Peace of Mind
Get the printable, Passover Soul Kit!**

101 Soul Tips, Easy Passover Recipes, Pesach Insights,
Meditations and Art Quotes
Get it here: www.holysparks.com/collections/holy-sparks-books-soul-kits

 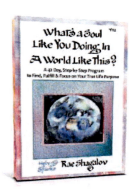 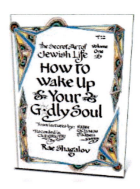

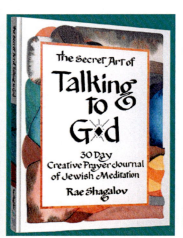

"The Secret Art of Talking to God"

"The Secret Art of Talking to God"
is a step-by-step introduction to Jewish prayer and meditation.
The beautiful art and calligraphy, guided meditations, and creative prayer journal prompts will inspire you to create a consistent, loving, intimate relationship with God in just 30 days.
Buy it on Amazon in hardcover, paperback or Kindle here:
http://bit.ly/talking-to-G-d

Made in the USA
San Bernardino, CA
25 July 2019